TALLIT

The Prayer Shawl"

Prayer, Faith, Power & Authority

by Stephanie Arrington

I thank God for His continuous grace on my life, and for considering me.

This book is dedicated to my literary agent, Marie Lewis before I was assigned my publishing agent at Christian Faith Publishers. You encouraged me to publish this book. Thank you for your support, words of encouragement, and just listening.

^{37} Again the L ORD spoke to Moses, saying, ^{38} "Speak to the children of Israel: Tell them to make tassels on the corners of their garments throughout their generations, and to put a blue thread in the tassels of the corners. ^{39} And you shall have the tassel, that you may look upon it and remember all the commandments of the L ORD and do them, and that you *may* not follow the harlotry to which your own heart and your own eyes are inclined, ^{40} and that you may remember and do all My commandments, and be holy for your God. ^{41} I *am* the L ORD your God, who brought you out of the land of Egypt, to be your God: I *am* the L ORD your God."

Numbers 15: 37-40 NKJV

Table of Contents

1
The Tallit

The tallit (also spelled tallis or talith) is a garment one can wear to create a sense of personal space during prayer - the name comes from two Hebrew words: TAL meaning tent and ITH meaning little.

Therefore, you have an etymology of LITTLE TENT. By wrapping yourself in it, or by covering your head with it, the intention and direction of your prayers can be enhanced. The tradition is that the tallit is worn only during the morning prayers, except for the Kol Nidre[1] service during Yom

---

[1] Kol Nidre is an Aramaic declaration recited in the synagogue before the beginning of the evening service on every Yom Kippur. It is not a prayer.

Kippur[2]. The garment can be made of linen, wool, silk or synthetics, so long as the biblical prohibition against the wearing of clothing combining linen and wool is observed.

It is not the garment itself, whether beautiful and adorned or plain and simple, that makes the prayer shawl special. What transforms a piece of cloth into a tallit are the tzitzit, the fringes on its four corners. The Torah instructs us to wear these fringes on the corners of our garments as a way of remembering and doing all God's commandments (Numbers 15:37-41). The mitzvah[3] is to remember God, to further holiness in our lives, and to keep the commandments, assisted by the visual reminder of the tzitzit. The tallit is therefore not worn at night because we are supposed to see the tzitzit by daylight.

---

[2]   Yom Kippur, also known as the Day of Atonement, is the holiest day of the year in Judaism. Its central themes are atonement and repentance.

[3]   Hebrew word meaning "commandment"

What is a tallit?

The tallit (also pronounced tallis) is a prayer shawl, the most authentic Jewish garment. The rectangular garment can be made of linen, wool, silk or synthetics, so long as the biblical prohibition against the wearing of clothing combining linen and wool is observed. It is made with special fringes called Tzitzit on each of the four corners. The purpose of the garment is to hold the Tzitzit.

Most tallit's (alternative plural: talleisim) have a neckband, called an Atarah[4], which most often has the blessing one recites when donning the tallit, embroidered across it.

Why wear a tallit?

The Lord said to Moses: Speak to the Israelites and instruct them to make for themselves fringes on the corners of their garments throughout the ages; let them attach a cord of blue to the fringe at each corner. That shall be your fringe; look at it and recall all the commandments of the Lord and observe them, so that you do not follow your heart and eyes in your lustful urge. Thus, you shall be reminded to observe all my commandments and to be holy to your God. I, the Lord, am your God, who brought you out of the land of

---

[4]   Hebrew meaning "crown"

Egypt to be your God: I, the Lord your God. (Numbers 15:37-41)

This scripture clearly describes the purpose of the tallit (garment) which is to hold the Tzizit (fringes), and the purpose of the Tzitzit (according to the Torah) is to remind us of God's commandments.

The tallit is worn for Morning Prayer, during the week as well as on Shabbat[5] and other holy days. It is not worn for afternoon and evening prayers because of the commandment that one should see the Tzitzit, which has been interpreted as meaning to be seen by the light of the day. The Shaliach Tzibur[6] usually wears a tallit, as well, even in the afternoon and evening.

Who wears a tallit?

Generally, a Jew who has reached the age of majority wear a tallit. In most communities, this is 13, though in some communities, girls reach the age of majority at 12. There exists a custom, not widely practiced, of not wearing a tallit prior to marriage: This custom was explained by the Maharil

---

[5]   Jewish Sabbath

[6]   Hebrew meaning messenger of a congregation in a public prayer, a Jewish prayer leader in the Synogogue also known as "Chazzon"

(Rabbi Yaacov Mollen, 1356-1427) based on the comparison of two verses in the Torah. The first, Deuteronomy 22:12 articulates the commandment concerning the wearing of tzitzit. It is followed by Deuteronomy 22:13, which says, "If a man takes a wife..." This custom is not widely practiced, however, in large measure because it prevents one from fulfilling a commandment between the age of 13 and the time one marries.

In congregations where a tallit is generally worn, you will find a rack of tallitot (plural) available for use by visitors near the entrance to the sanctuary.

Why does tallit have blue or black stripes?

The reason why the tallit is striped is simply because that was the fashion in Greece and Rome. But this doesn't answer the question of why blue or black? Tzitzis are supposed to include a thread of blue wool in each tassle. The stripes on the tallit remind us of the *'strand of techelet[7]'* once worn as part of the tzitzit. The Torah commands that tzitzis contain a thread of techelet.

---

[7]   Ancient Hebrew blue-violet. In modern Hebrew equivalent to light blue.

The color blue resembles the sea, the color of the sea resembles that of the sky and the sky is like the throne of God.

The dye used for this color came from an animal called the *Chilazone*. The Talmud recounts that the *Chilazone* appears only once in seventy years (Menachot 44a). Over the centuries, the exact identity of the Chilazone became forgotten. Hence, the '*strand of techelet*' became a mitzvah unable to fulfill (according to most authorities).

In memory of this dye, some adopted a custom to place a blue stripe on the garment itself. Others decided to add a black stripe of mourning for the lost element of the mitzvah. The black stripe gained popularity in Europe of the 15th through 19th centuries, when black-and-white clothing was more common for Jews in general. The blue stripe is now seeing a revival in the 20th and 21st centuries, but it's the older of the two customs. It just seems to us to be more modern.

How are the Tzitzit tied?

Tying Tzitzit is a Jewish art, a form of macrame[8]. A hole is carefully made and reinforced in each corner of the tallit.

---

[8]   A form of textile produced using knotting techniques

Through each hole, four strands are inserted: three short strands and one long strand. The longer stranded is called the shammash and this is the one which is used for winding around the others. To tie the Tzitzit, line up the four stands so that the three of equal length are doubled evenly, and the four strand is lined up at one end with the other seven ends. With four strands in one hand, and the other four in the other, make a double knot at the edge of the fabric.

Then take the shammash and wind it around the other seven strands seven times in a spiral motion. Make a second double knot, with four strands in one hand and four strands in the other. Then wind the shammash around the seven strands eight times and make another double knot. Wind the shammash around eleven times and make a double knot. Finally, wind the shammash thirteen times around the remaining seven strands and make one final double knot. When done correctly, the Tzitzit will have 7-8-11-13 winds between the double knots.

What does the 7-8-11-13 windings pattern mean?

There are several wonderful interpretations for this pattern of windings.

One interpretation is that each set of windings corresponds to one of the four letters in God's name.

Another interpretation employs Gematria[9], Jewish numerology, which assigns to each Hebrew letter a numeric value: aleph is 1, bet is 2, gimmel is 3, and so on. In this second interpretation of the windings of the Tzitzit, the numbers 7-8-11-13 have special meaning: 7+8=15, which in Hebrew is written yod-hay, the first two letters of God's name (Tetragrammaton[10]); 11=vav+hay, the third and fourth letters of God's name. Hence the first three windings "spell" God's holy name. Thirteen, the last set of windings, is equivalent in value to the word "echad" which means "one." Hence, all four windings can be interpreted to say, "God is one."

Yet another interpretation holds that when we consider the windings between the knots, 7, 8, 11, and 13, the first three numbers equal 26, which is numerically equivalent to the Tetragrammaton and the remaining number, 13, is equivalent to "echad". Therefore, the windings tell us that God is One. If we take the sum of the first three numbers (7+8+11) and equate that with God's Name, then the 13

---

[9]   a Kabbalistic method of interpreting the Hebrew scriptures by computing the numerical value of words, based on those of their constituent letters.

[10]   the Hebrew name of God transliterated in four letters as *YHWH* or *JHVH* and expressed as *Yahweh* or *Jehovah*.

which remain can also be interpreted to reflect the 13 attributes of God.

By still another interpretation, the Gematria value of the word "Tzitzit" (tzadi-yod-tzitzit-yod-taf) is 600. To this we add the eight strands plus the five knots, totaling 613 in all. According to tradition, God gave us 613 mitzvot (commandments) in the Torah. Just looking at the tallit with its Tzitzit, therefore, reminds us of the commandments, as the Torah says, "You should see them and remember all God's commandments and do them."

Each Tzitzit is made from 8 strings, 7 white and one blue. 'Seven' is the number representing perfection in the physical realm. 'Eight', therefore, transcends the physical realm and symbolizes a direct link to the spiritual realm.

Each group of 8 strings is knotted 5 times to form a Tzitzit. There are five books in the Torah.

Each of the 4 tzitzit have 8 strings, making a total of 32 strings. Thirty-two is the numeric value of the Hebrew word for "HEART". The tzitzit's loose strings represent God's 'heart strings'.

How to put on a Tallit

1. Open the tallit and hold in both hands so you can see atarah (the collar band on which the blessing is often embroidered.

2. Recite the berachah (blessing)

3. Kiss the end of atarah where the last word of the blessing is embroidered, and then and beginning where the first word is.

4. Wrap the tallit around your shoulders, holding it over your head for a moment of private meditation.

5. Adjust the tallit on your shoulders comfortably.

2
The Tradition

Customs of wearing a tallit

1. If you borrow the tallit for the service, say the deberachah

2. If you use it just for an aliyah[11], no need to say the berachah

---

[11] The Hebrew word translated as "elevation" or "going up". Also, being called up to the Torah reading and going up to Israel. (Genesis 50:1-14)

3. Don't take it into the bathroom

4. If you take the tallit off for a short time (e.g. to go
    to the bathroom) you don't need to repeat the
    berachah when putting it on again.

Kissing the tzitzit

There are several times during the service when people kiss
the tzitzit symbolically. First is during the recitation of the
third paragraph of the Shema[12] (Numbers 15:37-41) which
mentions the tzitzit three times. As the worshiper reads the
word "tzitzit," it is customary to kiss the tzitzit, which were
gathered together in one hand prior to reciting the Shema.

---

[12]   A prayer. Also, the first two words of a section of the Torah or
the title. i.e. Deut 6:4 "Hear O Israel"

(First and Main Part of the Shema)

וְאָהַבְתָּ אֵת יהוה אֱלֹהֶיךָ	You shall love Adonai your God
בְּכָל לְבָבְךָ וּבְכָל נַפְשְׁךָ	with all your heart, with all your soul,
וּבְכָל מְאֹדֶךָ	and with all your might.
וְהָיוּ הַדְּבָרִים הָאֵלֶּה	And these words
אֲשֶׁר אָנֹכִי מְצַוְּךָ הַיּוֹם	which I command you today
עַל לְבָבֶךָ	shall be in your heart.
וְשִׁנַּנְתָּם לְבָנֶיךָ	You shall teach them diligently to your children
וְדִבַּרְתָּ בָּם	and you shall speak of them
בְּשִׁבְתְּךָ בְּבֵיתֶךָ	when you are sitting at home
וּבְלֶכְתְּךָ בַדֶּרֶךְ	and when you go on a journey,
וּבְשָׁכְבְּךָ	when you lie down
וּבְקוּמֶךָ.	and when you rise up.
וּקְשַׁרְתָּם לְאוֹת עַל יָדֶךָ	You shall bind them as a sign on your hand
וְהָיוּ לְטֹטָפֹת בֵּין עֵינֶיךָ	and they shall be jewels between your eyes
וּכְתַבְתָּם עַל מְזֻזוֹת	You shall inscribe them on the doorposts
בֵּיתֶךָ וּבִשְׁעָרֶיךָ.	of your house and on your gates

Deuteronomy 6:5-9

When the Torah is removed from the Ark and carried around the synagogue in a Hakafah (procession), those within reach touch the Torah mantle with tzitzit (if they are wearing a tallit) or a siddur (prayer book) if they are not. They then kiss the tzitzit or siddur which touched the Torah scroll. This is an expression of love and affection for the great gift which Torah is to the people.

Jews were commanded in the book of Leviticus to wear a fringed garment. When you look at it, you shall remember my law and remember me. Did you ever tie a string around your finger to remember something? Well, God said, "tie a string around your garment and when you look at it, you can remember me". Now, since Jews were supposed to remember God's Law with the fringes, they are tied in a certain way. There were 5 books of Moses, and so the fringe has 5 knots. So, that reminds us of God's Law. God's name in Hebrew is a word Jews never pronounce: Y H W H (Yahweh). God's name has 4 letters. Since the fringe has 5 knots, there are 4 spaces between them. Consequently, when a Jew looks at the fringe, he remembers God's Law and God's name. That is the Jewish

significance of the fringe. Here is the Christian meaning.

We recall the woman who had an issue of blood for twelve

years. She approached Jesus. Many translations say that

she touched the hem of his garment. That is a bad

translation. Rather, she touched the fringes of his garment

and thereby she was touching God's word and God's name.

God's Law and God's name is what the fringe symbolizes.

Not the hem of a skirt. The fringe symbolizes Jesus

himself. The Word and the name.

3
Biblical *Tallit*
(The Four Cornered Garment)

The *Tallit* as the visible symbol of the Word of God is a
demonstration of the positional and personal power that is
transferred when the mantle passes. In all subsequent
generations, the term passing the mantle has come to mean
the transfer of authority and anointing from one leader to
another, from one generation to another.

Colors on the *Tallit* were usually crimson purple and royal blue as outlined in the Torah for the High Priest.

Levitical Tribe has the colors of the Blood Red, has white & black stripes in it, and are also in the banners of the tribes.

Little Tent

The *Tallit* is known as a prayer shawl or little tent because it can be worn over you like a little tent.

Only men were obligated to wear them. Women could wear them if they wanted to.

The under garment or robe was called a HALUK, which was of lighter weight. The outer garment was the *Tallit* and it was of heavier weight. There were other outer garments that were worn as well. One was the me'il, which was a cloak or robe. It was exclusively used by men of rank or of the priestly order. Samuel's annual ritual robe as a child was a me'il (I Sam 2:19). Jonathan's uniform cloak was a me'il (I Sam 18:4). The corner of Saul's me'il was cut off by David (I Sam 24:4). A me'il was worn by King David's daughters (II Sam 13:18). David and the Levites dressed in fine linen me'ils during a procession celebrating the transport of the ark to Jerusalem (I Chron 15:27). Ezra tore his me'il, along with his clothing (Ezra 9:3,5). Job and his friends tore their me'ils in grief (Job 1,2). Other examples or symbols of the me'il are, Job clothed in a me'il of righteousness (Job 29). Clothed in a me'il of shame (Psalm 109). Zeal as a cloak (Isaiah 59:17). Robe of righteousness (Isaiah 61:10). Princes of the sea shall lay down their robes (Ezekiel 26:16). [Strong's 4598].

Psalms 61:4 "Let me dwell in your tent forever! Let me take refuge under the shelter of your wings!" Selah

The Tallit As a 'Closet'

Greek word for closet is *tameion*, which means "an inner chamber, or a secret room." The closeting of oneself in the covering of the Tallit (prayer shawl) was a symbolic separation from the world.

> *"But when you pray, go into your room and shut the door and pray to your Father who is in secret. And your Father who sees in secret will reward you." Matt 6:6*

4
Most Notable Scripture of Jesus' Garment

Matt 9:20 And behold, a woman, who had a flow of blood for twelve years, came up behind Him and touched the hem of His garment.

Jesus being a Jew would have observed the law and worn a tallit.

Q. Who was this woman that touched Jesus?

This woman was someone who was broken and considered an outcast due to her condition. Because of her condition she was not allowed in the Temple or touch anyone for that matter. She spent all her money on doctors but to no avail. All she had left was faith, knowing that if she could get close enough to Jesus, she would be made whole.

Q. What is the Biblical Reference to all the people believing that if they touched Jesus garment, they would be healed?

Jesus had been on the Eastern side of Galilee, which was primarily a Gentile area. Now He is traveling near His home on the western side of the Sea of Galilee. A story is circulating clear across the lake about this man being Jesus with healing power.

> **Matthews Gospel chapter 14:34-36 ...*And when they had crossed over, they came to land at Gennesaret.*
> *v.35 And when the men of that place recognized him, they sent around to all that region and brought to him all who were sick*
> *v. 36 and implored him that they might only touch the fringe of his garment. And as many as touched it were made well.***

The hem of His garment was where these fringes were. These four tassels were worn by the Jews and identified them as such and that they were apart of God's chosen ones. Every time this garment was worn, it was to remind him that they belonged to God. This scripture also describes to us that Jesus dressed as the people of His time did.

The disciples and some others were on their way to the great healing service, or some type of revival service, when something unusual happened.

Matthew 9:20-22 … *And behold, a woman who had suffered from a discharge of blood for twelve years came up behind him and touched the fringe of his garment,*
v.21 for she said to herself, "If I only touch his garment, I will be made well."
v. 22 Jesus turned, and seeing her he said, "Take heart, daughter; your faith has made you well." And instantly the woman was made well.

5
More Key Pieces of the Story

Luke 8:42-43... *for he had an only daughter, about twelve years of age, and she was dying. As Jesus went, the people pressed around him.*
v. 43 And there was a woman who had had a discharge of blood for twelve years, and though she had spent all her living on physicians, she could not be healed by anyone.

New fact, doctors could not heal her or do anything for twelve years. I imagine her funds were a little bit low at this point.

Luke says that the crowds were so massive they were almost crushing Jesus, crowding in trying to get around Him.

Matthew basically says that a lady slipped up behind Him. She had to do a little bit of pushing and shoving maybe to get through the crowd.

Many times, when we envision this woman with an issue, we somehow in our mind think that she was all decrepit and bent down walking through the crowd and the only reason she touched the edge of His garment is because she was bent over due to back issues. Scripture didn't say anything about that only that she had an issue of blood.

Q. So why is this woman moving through this crowd?

It was her faith that moved her toward her healing. Her desperation, character and inner desire for survival all are elements of her character and faith.

Q. Why does she come there and push through them, why doesn't she call His name out now?

Her "condition" didn't allow her to, and she didn't want anything or anyone to stop her from getting what she has waited twelve years to receive. Her healing. Not only will she receive a divine miraculous healing, but a close personal relationship with Jesus. He will not only touch her body, but her heart and soul as well.

Q. What was she saying within herself?

If I can only get close enough to touch Jesus, I have faith to know and believe I will never be the same again.

> Let us look at Luke 8:44-46 which says, *she came up behind him and touched the fringe of his garment, and immediately her discharge of blood ceased.*
> ***v. 45 And Jesus said, "Who was it that touched me?" When all denied it, Peter said, "Master, the crowds surround you and are pressing in on you!"***
> ***v. 46 But Jesus said, "Someone touched me, for I perceive that power has gone out from me."***

Everyone is there and they are all pressing in and when He says, "who touched me", Peter and the others that was with him proclaimed, "Master, the people are crowding and pressing against you." But Jesus said, I perceive someone have touched me for the virtue is gone out of me.

So basically, what they are saying yes someone touched you, look at the crowd, can't you see they're pressing in. But Jesus says, no this was a different type of touch. Someone touched the *Power in Me.* And the Power in Me was released.

Luke 8:47 continues the story…

And when the woman saw that she was not hidden, she came trembling, and falling down before him and declared in the presence of all the people why she had touched him, and how she had been immediately healed.

 Then the woman realized she could not go un-noticed. Picture this, she is touching the hem of His garment which we need to see what that really is. She is bending down to touch His garment, and she's probably lower than everyone else, and Peter is saying, "What do you mean someone touched you?" "Can't you see everybody around?"

Then she kind of looks up and realizes there's no way out. Even though she said within herself, "If I may but touch his garment, I shall be whole" (Matthew 9:21). As we read this portion of bible scripture, we have 3 different accounts of the woman with the issue of blood, but in all accounts this woman is anonymous. Matthew's account tells us that Jesus turned and saw her, Mark's and Luke's account tells us that Jesus knowing that virtue left him asked the question, "who touched me"?

Even though she pressed in the crowd of unruly men that were all excited to be with Jesus, she knows she has been caught. Most likely she did not fear Jesus' reaction but the crowd. You see if she had been bleeding for twelve years the Hebrew scripture says she is unclean; in fact, she is supposed to announce to everyone that she is unclean.

Wow, one touch of Jesus has made her clean and acceptable. Also, consider that Jesus had not died upon the Cross yet and that His redemptive Blood had not yet been shed. So, when the woman touched Him, the transfer happened through her faith. He stopped what He was doing to respond to that act of faith. Remember Jesus only did what He saw the Father doing. How awesome is His Mercy?

Touching this woman would render anyone unclean. You cannot go into the Temple. It won't matter if you're a priest, it won't matter if you're the High Priest, and it won't matter if you're the common person. If you touch an unclean person, you are considered unclean. Being considered unclean your connection with God is broken.

So, this woman has lived with a social stigma…What courage it took for her to go into that crowd. That's faith!

She is breaking some social and religious taboos. Basically, she has rendered a bunch in the crowd, unclean. So, she knows she's caught, it's one of those moments when everybody's quiet.

> **Luke 8:47** *And when the woman saw that she was not hidden, she came trembling, and falling before him declared in the presence of all the people why she had touched him, and how she had been immediately healed.*

IN THE PRESENCE OF ALL THE PEOPLE

> **Matt 9:22** *Jesus turned, and seeing her he said, "Take heart, daughter; your faith has made you well." And instantly the woman was made well.*

6
The Foundation of the Garment

NUMBERS 15: 37-41 The LORD said to Moses,

v. 38 "Speak to the people of Israel and tell them to make tassels on the corners of their garments throughout their generations, and to put a cord of blue on the tassel of each corner.

v. 39 And it shall be a tassel for you to look at and remember all the commandments of the LORD, to do them, not to follow after your own heart and your own eyes, which you are inclined to whore after.

v. 40 so you shall remember and do all my commandments and be holy to your God.

v. 41 I am the LORD your God, who brought you out of the land of Egypt to be your God: I am the LORD your God."

You will find out that the Hebrews were commanded to make this Biblical garment with four corners, to attach fringes or tzizit. The long fringe knotted in a particular way. The Biblical version says there needs to be at least one blue cord or one blue string inside of it and that identifies it.

Remember the Jews were commanded to eat certain things and not eat certain things. To dress certain ways and to not dress other ways.

All of this was just a visual reminder of setting them apart, sanctifying them. A visual announcement or reminder to those around them that these are a particular people, these are peculiar people.

These are people that God is using for a special mission. Because they live in a world where there are:

- All kinds of ways to dress.
- All kinds of ways to eat.
- All kinds of ways to worship.
- All kinds of ways to speak.

God Himself carved them out from all the people, making them a distinct people.

Sometimes when we read the OT, we read the 613 laws; Many times, Christians say well, we're under grace now, not under law. That is true, however if you would read most of the 613 Biblical commandments in the Torah (first five books of the Bible) you will find that you (Christians) keep them without thinking about it, because it's more than just not stealing. It talks about what if one of my animals injures someone else's animals. It talks about how we work out this faith when this happens.

However, this garment was commanded of God.

The tassels or *tzitzit* as they are called in Hebrew look like this:

Some New Testament translations put this Hebrew word into Greek, and then into English; the translation is different. It is translated as 'hem of His garment'. The hem for us is like what is at the bottom of our pants, or at the edge of our sleeve. Folded over and sewn to avoid fraying.

That is not what's talked about in scripture, what was talked about was that the woman touched His (Jesus) *tzizit,* the fringe.

Q. Now why did she do that? Why did she touch the fringe?

Tzitzit and Tallit

They shall make themselves tzitzit on the corners of their garments throughout their generations, and they shall place on the tzitzit of each corner a thread of techeilet. And it shall be tzitzit for you, and you will see it, and you will remember all the mitzvot of the L-RD and do them and not follow your heart or your eyes and run after them. -Numbers 15:38-40

The Torah commands us to wear tzitzit (fringes) at the corners of our garments as a reminder of the mitzvot. The passage also instructs that the fringe should have a thread of "techeilet," believed to be a blue or turquoise dye, but the source of that dye is no longer known, so tzitzit are today are all white. There is a complex procedure for tying the knots of the tzitzit, filled with religious and numerological significance.

The mitzvah to wear tzitzit applies only to four-cornered garments, which were common in biblical times but are not common anymore. To fulfill this mitzvah, adult men wear a four-cornered shawl called a tallit during morning services, along with the tefillin (plural)[13] (pictured above).

In some Orthodox congregations, only married men wear a tallit; in others, both married and unmarried men wear one. In Conservative, Reform and Reconstructionist

---

[13]	A set of small black leather boxes containing scrolls of parchment inscribed with verses from the Torah. The arm tefillah or shel yad is placed on the upper arm and the straps wrapped around the arm, hand and fingers. And the head tafillah or shel rosh is placed above the forehead.

synagogues, both men and women may wear a tallit, but men are somewhat more likely than women to do so. A blessing is recited when you put on the tallit.

7
The History of the Garment

There are three important things to remember about these tassels in particular. They are a mixture of Linen & Wool (which testified that the people had some connection to the priesthood, because of the wool)

> Realize you may not be called to be the "Pastor", you may not be called to be the "evangelist" or the "prophet" or the "teacher" but you have a connection to the ministry because everyone is called to share the Good News of Jesus Christ.

Some of our <u>roles</u> are different, but those in the five-fold are here to equip the others to do the Work of the Lord. Different job specifications, but all of us have a connection to the ministry. This means full participation, not just watching from the side lines.

Wool thread is in the tassels. The wool comes from a sheep or a lamb which testified their connection to the sacrificial system, the sacrificial lamb. Wool in the tassel was a reminder of the sacrifice and the atonement and the substitution of an animal for their sin. Jesus, The Lamb of God, who take away the sins of the world, is the ultimate sacrifice (Isaiah 53:7).

The Blue thread reminded them of their connection to royalty. Not everyone wore the blue, only those most wealthy of the pagan world would have had this royal blue color.

> Blue is also the color of our sky, making a connection or physical reminder for the ancient people of the residence of God, in the Heavenlies. The blue tassel reminds them of their Royal connection and the Biblical commandment to the Torah.

The color is not important, just the purpose. The other colors are for our preference.

Even the prayer before you put on your prayer
shawl doesn't have to be present.

The whole purpose of the *Tallit (prayer shawl)* is to hold
the fringe on the corners as a reminder to the people about
God. That they have been set aside, sanctified and made
Holy unto God.

What is the significance of the Four Tassels?

Q. What is the reason for the four cornered garments, why
are there four and not three?

In Biblical times the four corners and the tassels
represented certain things.

There is no particular order to the top corner
or the bottom left corner, or any of that. The
corners remember them.

#1 The *Tallit (prayer shawl)* had a family connection. It
represented their Identity. Even in certain families that tie
these they have their own way. Like a signature card. When

you would see a particular fringe, you could tell who tied it. What family it came from. It was the family signature.

#2 Status within the tribe or the community was represented in the tying of the tassels. This was becoming a problem in Jesus time.

Luke 20:45-47 Jesus made a comment as they were watching people enter the House of Prayer and He said "Oh, the Pharisees love to stand with their long flowing robes, so everybody will see them praying and worshipping God". So, they forgot the purpose of the tzitzit. The Pharisees would make their tzitzit longer and add more blue in it, because then you know they were wealthy. Pride!

A way of saying, because you poor folks can't afford this much blue. Look at me. Even though the more ostentatious Pharisees made show of their alms, giving their public prayers, the greater percentage of the Pharisees were sincere in their separation and secreting themselves in prayer so that with *kavanah* (proper attitude and concentration) they approached God and entered into a knowing relationship with Him.

· The higher the status and the higher your social structure of the day the longer and more elaborate your tassels would be. Because of this costly blue, it signified a status.

There is another history that goes along with it. Remember when David was being chased by Saul, and he didn't have as many men as Saul, but Saul was determined that he was going to kill him. Saul went into the cave into the inter recesses of the cave to sleep and was guarded by all his men. We know David was in there. During the night David sneaks over the ravine and instead of killing Saul he cuts the edge of his garment, and he took the tzizit, because everyone would know what King Saul's would look like. So, the next day when David is on the other side of the hill, the mountain with the ravine, he calls out to Saul. Saul is telling David how much he is going to kill him, and David basically says "Saul, look at your garment, I could have killed you, but I tried to respect your authority. So, look at this tassel I have it as a symbol of your authority and one of yours is missing"

· So, it is a symbol of AUTHORITY.

Because it represented authority many people missed this piece. When a prophet had a Word to give to the king, he would inscribe that prophesy or press his seal into the tzizit in a particular pattern, as if to say 'this is official' (this would be similar to the wax seal used on fine stationary). Melted wax was placed on the back of an envelope and the monogram pressed into that wax. This actually came from the practice started with these tassels. Last thing represented in the tassels, is the Priestly purity or power. It was a reminder of personal Holiness.

The Tassels

4 tassels, one on each corner. 8 strands – 1 tassel – 5 knots – 4 windings.
That = 18 the numeric symbolism to chai/life

1 numeric equivalent of that is Echad meaning the Lord YHWH, He is one God.

4 windings are a numeric equivalent of that which was taken out of the covenant name.
Now there is a series of 4 windings.

5 knots are symbolic to the first five books of Moses; the Torah.
Genesis/Exodus/Leviticus/Numbers/Deuteronomy

(1st-7)

(2nd-8)

(3rd-11)

(4th -13)

These all add up to 39

which is the number of stripes Jesus took {Isaiah 53:5} By *His stripes we are healed...*

Malachi 4:2-3 But for you who fear my name, the sun of righteousness shall rise with healing in its wings. You shall go out leaping like calves from the stall.

v. 3 And you shall tread down the wicked, for they will be ashes under the soles of your feet, on the day when I act, says the LORD of hosts.

8

The Issue: There is More to Her Story

Q. So what happened to this woman with an issue of Blood?

She made a divine connection with the One that could heal her and make her whole. It was by faith that she made the connection. When she said if I could only touch the hem of His garment, I will be made whole, she was also saying if I touch His power and authority, I will never be the same again. She was transformed. *This means that anyone who belongs to Christ has become a new person. The old life is gone, a new life has begun (2 Corinthians 5:17)*

Q. Why did he call her a daughter?

As a daughter of Abraham (Luke 13:16) her faith is acknowledged and honored by Jesus. It was not faith without a touch or a touch without faith. It was the right time for Him to show endearment toward her. It was appropriate that He recognized her as His own.

"But without faith it is impossible to please him, for he that comes to God must believe that he is, and that he is a rewarder of them that diligently seek him." Hebrews 11:6

Q. And why did she touch His fringe?

It is indicated that during Jesus time, during the first century there was a scripture in Zechariah that talks about there is healing in His wings. Many believe that the fringe on the bottom of the prayer shawl is what is being referred to as the "wings" and that there would be healing in His wings.

"But unto you that fear my name shall the Sun of righteousness rise with healing in his wings, and ye shall go forth, and grow up as calves of the stall."
Malachi 4:2

Q. Why is this important in connection with Jesus?

The reason why it is important with Jesus is because of all the people that day, this woman actually knew who He was! Because the belief was, "you know how there will be a true Messiah? There will be healing in His wings"

Q. What was it Jesus said in the midst of everybody pressing into Him?

"Who touched Me?" "Power has gone out of Me"

She touched one of the corners, one of the hems, one of the fringes, One of the Tzizit.   Also, she touched His Authority. She connected with His status. She connected with His Purity.   She knew His TRUE identity. The *"True Messiah will have Healing in His wings"*

This anonymous woman spent her whole life trying to get healed. It was a male dominated society. She was unclean. She was an outcast. In scriptures Luke tells us that no doctor could do anything for her. This is a woman that for twelve years carried a burden on her own shoulder. We don't even hear about her family or even know if she had a family. If you can't stop bleeding guess what, your husband is going to get rid of you, because you're going to render him unclean. The neighbors are going to talk saying, "why are you still with that woman, don't you know that she's just filthy and unclean?" We don't want her in our neighborhood (REJECTION) and ladies she cannot come to the well, to get the water when you come. People are talking about her, when she walks down the street, and

most of the time she has her head down. She's
embarrassed to make eye contact with people, because
they're always saying something about her behind her back
and to her face. Pointing at her, just like today when we
see somebody that don't fit our status quo. She didn't even
need to think about going near the Temple because she was
not welcome in a place of worship. You are not welcome at
the place of prayer, because you have something wrong
with you. Somehow in her heart she knew who HE really
was. Everyone else was there for the fish & bread.
Everyone else may have been there for the mob psychology
of the crowd. She wasn't interested in these things; she said
in her heart "if I could only touch His garment", His tzitzit,
I would be healed. Scripture says that as soon as she did
that, she was healed instantly. And the blood stopped
flowing.

When she was caught, and everyone was looking at her, she
shared with them why she did what she did. The Bible
doesn't let us exactly what she says, but Jesus lets us know
when He turns to her and says "Daughter, your faith has
made you whole".

Q. Why did He say that?

This woman with the issue of blood was not a relative of Jesus.

Even today, but especially in Biblical times only if you were a wife or a daughter you could touch the 'Tallit (prayer shawl)' but if you weren't family, the daughter or the wife you could not touch. It was not allowed. So not only is this woman unclean, she is touching a man she is not related to. This woman just doesn't understand the rules of the day. But, maybe she did, but she was in a position of desperation and this was her chance to live again. It was her faith that healed her.

The grace and mercy of Jesus let's everyone else know when this woman touched Him. Power and virtue left Him because the woman knows who Jesus is.

To touch Jesus brings you into remembrance of His identity. When you touch Jesus, you take hold of His Power. When you touch Jesus, you take hold of His purity. When you take hold of His identity you know who you are and He will give you the proper status, and you will know what it means to be a child of the King. The Lord of Lords. So, it is up to you to choose which identity you want.

Do you want the identity that the world gives you or do you want the identity that He sends, that you are a peculiar person, that you are fearfully and wonderfully made, that you are an overcomer, that you are not defeated?

It's all up to you. Sometimes we must touch who He really is. Regardless of what the crowd says to us.

There is a Hebrew word *Kanaph* which means wings can also mean corner.

Jews have recognized the fact that God's law symbolized in the tzizit of their prayer shawls is their guardian. Just as the Tallit surrounds the praying Jew, so God surrounds His people. "We can contend in a spiritual sense, that when putting on the Tallit that it separates us and shield us from outside distractions and from foreign thoughts. The Tallit surrounds and symbolizes protection."

Exodus 19:4, "You yourselves have seen what I did to the Egyptians, and how I bore you on eagles' wings and brought you to myself".

When a Jewish man wraps himself in his Tallit, he

symbolically places himself under God's sheltering love. Indeed, when he does the Tallit, he recites Psalms 36:7, 9. This material action gives new and more meaning to Psalms 57:1 declaration: "In the shadow of thy wings will I make my refuge."

The Ark of the Covenant that was the focal point of the "Most Holy Place" in both the tabernacle in the wilderness and the Temple in Jerusalem, demonstrates the fact that even God's throne itself is overshadowed by the wings of divine protection. The mercy seat on the top of the Ark of the Covenant was the site of the localized material manifestation of the Spirit of God, the *Shekhinah*, covering the four corners of the mercy seat were the wings of two cherubim. What powerful imagery: God's provision of mercy and loving kindness for His people is always overshadowed and protected by the wings of the "living creatures" that both guard His throne and extend perpetual, unceasing worship that extols His Holiness: "*Kadosh, Kadosh, Kadosh*" (HOLY, HOLY, HOLY)

The testimony to God's ancient people (and to His people of all ages) is that His mercies are unending, extending to the age of ages. Those in the Messiah are "seated with

Christ in Heavenly places, "enfolded in the wings of His everlasting mercies.

Quoting from Psalms 36:7 this prayer suggests the full significance of the Tallit:

"How precious is thy loving-kindness, O God! And under the shadow of thy wings so the children of men take shelter…"

As you cover yourself with the Tallit, you have a physical symbolic awareness of the fact that you are secure in the shadow of God's presence. Being "under the wings" of the Almighty.

"When you put on a Tallit you should think that the light of the infinite One is hidden within the Tallit that you wrap yourself in, and that when the wings of the Tallit cover you, you are covered in the wings of the light of the Infinite One." In His divine protection.

9
Let Us Pray

Thank You Heavenly Father for covering us in your tender mercies and everlasting loving kindness~ Quicken my heart now to know my identity in You, my new status and right standing in Your Righteousness. Begin to heal me Lord, physically, emotionally and Spiritually. Create in me a clean heart and renew in me a right Spirit. I thank you for understanding of this healing You brought forth for the woman with the issue. Touch me Lord and I too shall be made whole.

In Jesus Name~ Amen.

References

Holy Bible King James Version (2000). *Holman Bible Publishers.*

Holy Bible King James Amplified Version (1995). *The Zondervan Corporation and the Lockman Foundation*

Wikipedia, *Tallit.* 29 September 2010. http://en.wikipedia.org/wiki/Tallit

"Tallit: Jewish Prayer Shawl". Religion Facts. 26 February 2005. Updated 4 March 2006. Accesses 22 October 2010. http://www.religionfacts.com/Judaism/things/tallit.htm

"Tallit-Prayer Shawl Tallith". Judaica Guide. 2005-2010. http://www.judaica-guide.com/tallit/

Matthew Henry's Commentary on the Whole Bible (1991). *Hendricks Publishers.*

Strong, James. Strong's Complete Dictionary of Bible Words (1996). *Thomas Nelson Publishers.*

The Word in Life Study Bible NKJV. "Just a Reminder-Numbers 15:37-41 Thomas Nelson Publishers, 1993.

"The Tallit-A Most Genuine Jewish Garment". Jewish-Art.org.2006-2010. http://www.jewish-art.org/tallit.html

Eerdmans Dictionary of the Bible (2000). *Wm. B. Eerdmans Publishing Company.*